This bo

CH00055111

Gift

From

....

To

....

Date

....

May God bless you through this book

Prayers to retain your pregnancy

PRAYERS TO RETAIN YOUR PREGNANCY

PRAYERS TO RETAIN YOUR PREGNANCY

Copyright © 2014

PRAYER M. MADUEKE

ISBN: 1500165913

Prayer Publications

First Edition, 2014

For further information of permission

1 Babatunde close, off Olaitan Street, Surulere, Lagos, Nigeria
+234 803 353 0599
Email: pastor@prayermadueke.com,
Website: www.prayermadueke.com

Dedication

This book is dedicated to women who are trusting God to protect their babies in the womb until delivery. The Lord who sees your sincere dedication will answer your prayers Amen.

Prayers to retain your pregnancy

BOOK OVERVIEW

PRAYERS TO RETAIN YOUR PREGNANCY

- *Guard your pregnancy*
- *Put on the whole armor of God*
- *Powers that terminate pregnancies*

GUARD YOUR PREGNANCY

In this world of increasing complexities, even in the midst of breakthrough scientific and medical inventions, many pregnant women continue to struggle to retain their pregnancies. In this book, I will reveal to you how Satan labors to destroy many pregnancies, in order to equip you with the Word of God on how to guard your pregnancy.

The scripture revealed that the world is a battleground. The war is between good and evil; between God's children and Satan's agents.

> *"For we wrestle not against flesh and blood, but against principalities, against powers, against the rulers of the darkness of this world, against spiritual wickedness in high places"* (Ephesians 6:12).

> *"Fight the good fight of faith, lay hold on eternal life, where unto thou art also called, and hast professed a good profession before many witnesses"* (1 Timothy 6:12).

> *"For though we walk in the flesh, we do not war after the flesh: (For the weapons of our warfare are not carnal, but mighty through God to the pulling down of strong holds;) Casting down imaginations, and every high thing that exalteth itself against the knowledge of God, and bringing into captivity every thought to the obedience of Christ"* (2 Corinthians 10:3-5).

Every human alive is involved in spiritual warfare and only true believers know how to achieve real victory in the Word of God. Being ignorant of these spiritual conflicts would prove very costly. The first defeat all humans suffer on earth is the curse of the sin of Adam, which puts all humanity into slavery.

> *"Now we know that what things soever the law saith, it saith to them who are under the law: that every mouth may be stopped, and all the world may become guilty before God"* (<u>Romans 3:19</u>).

> *"[18]He that believeth on him is not condemned: but he that believeth not is condemned already, because he hath not believed in the name of the only begotten Son of God. [36] He that believeth on the Son hath everlasting life: and he that believeth not the Son shall not see life; but the wrath of God abideth on him"* (<u>John 3:18</u>, <u>36</u>).

> *"Behold, I was shapen in iniquity; and in sin did my mother conceive me"* (<u>Psalms 51:5</u>).

Many people live under the power of sin without knowing how to escape. They were born into sin, they lived and died in sin without receiving deliverance and salvation. They lived under the oppression of the devil and never reigned over any circumstance in their lives.

> *"For the Son of man is come to seek and to save that which was lost"* (<u>Luke 19:10</u>).

> *"And saying, The time is fulfilled, and the kingdom of God is at hand: repent ye, and believe the gospel"* (<u>Mark 1:15</u>).

> *"For by grace are ye saved through faith; and that not of yourselves: it is the gift of God: Not of works, lest any man should boast"* (<u>Ephesians 2:8-9</u>).

On the cross of Calvary, Jesus Christ paid the full price for our freedom. Christ's death brought deliverance for us and destined us to overcome sin, Satan, evil spirits and all problems in life. The devil is the cause of all sicknesses, afflictions and problems. He uses sin to bring people into problems and bondage. Problems enter into people's lives through sins they commit or inherit. However, if you repent, confess your sins and forsake them, you can resist the devil and he will flee. Christians have power over the devil and all his works. Praise God!

> *"And he said unto them, I beheld Satan as lightning fall from heaven. Behold, I give unto you power to tread on serpents and scorpions, and over all the power of the enemy: and nothing shall by any means hurt you. Notwithstanding in this rejoice not, that the spirits are subject unto you; but rather rejoice, because your names are written in heaven"* (Luke 10: 18-20)

> *"Then he called his twelve disciples together, and gave them power and authority over all devils, and to cure diseases"* (Luke 9:1).

> *"He that committeth sin is of the devil; for the devil sinneth from the beginning. For this purpose the Son of God was manifested, that he might destroy the works of the devil"* (1 John 3:8).

However, if you desire for true deliverance, then do away with sin. Even after overcoming sin, if you do not resist the devil, he will come back to oppress you. Jesus has to heal the sick and deliver the oppressed by rebuking the devil and casting out the evil spirit that caused the sickness.

> *"As they went out, behold, they brought to him a dumb man possessed with a devil. And when the devil was cast out, the dumb spake: and the*

multitudes marvelled, saying, It was never so seen in Israel" (<u>Matthew 9:32-33</u>).

"And when they were come to the multitude, there came to him a certain man, kneeling down to him, and saying, Lord, have mercy on my son: for he is lunatic, and sore vexed: for ofttimes he falleth into the fire, and oft into the water. And I brought him to thy disciples, and they could not cure him. Then Jesus answered and said, O faithless and perverse generation, how long shall I be with you? How long shall I suffer you? Bring him hither to me. And Jesus rebuked the devil; and he departed out of him: and the child was cured from that very hour. Then came the disciples to Jesus apart, and said, Why could not we cast him out? And Jesus said unto them, Because of your unbelief: for verily I say unto you, If ye have faith as a grain of mustard seed, ye shall say unto this mountain, Remove hence to yonder place; and it shall remove; and nothing shall be impossible unto you. Howbeit this kind goeth not out but by prayer and fasting" (<u>Matthew 17:14-21</u>).

"Was returning, and sitting in his chariot read Esaias the prophet. Then the Spirit said unto Philip, Go near, and join thyself to this chariot. And Philip ran thither to him, and heard him read the prophet Esaias, and said, Understandest thou what thou readest? And he said, How can I, except some man should guide me? And he desired Philip that he would come up and sit with him. The place of the scripture which he read was this, He was led as a sheep to the slaughter; and like a lamb dumb before his shearer, so opened he not his mouth: In his humiliation his judgment was taken away: and who shall declare his generation? For his life is taken from the earth. And the eunuch answered

Philip, and said, I pray thee, of whom speaketh the prophet this? Of himself, or of some other man?" (Acts 8:28-34).

Jesus casted them out by the Spirit of God and the same Spirit of God lives in us. We can cast out the devil and conduct deliverance like the one Jesus did. The Scripture confirmed this:

"And these signs shall follow them that believe; In my name shall they cast out devils; they shall speak with new tongues; They shall take up serpents; and if they drink any deadly thing, it shall not hurt them; they shall lay hands on the sick, and they shall recover" (Mark 16:17-18).

Salvation or being born-again cannot remove all stubborn demons from us. We need to confront them as we work out our salvation with fear and trembling (*See* Philippians 2:12).

"But I see another law in my members, warring against the law of my mind, and bringing me into captivity to the law of sin which is in my members" (Romans 7:23).

"And after those days his wife Elisabeth conceived, and hid herself five months, saying, Thus hath the Lord dealt with me in the days wherein he looked on me, to take away my reproach among men. And in the sixth month the angel Gabriel was sent from God unto a city of Galilee, named Nazareth" (Luke 1:24-26).

"Submit yourselves therefore to God. Resist the devil, and he will flee from you" (James 4:7).

The battle will rage on until Jesus returns, and only those who received Christ and lean on the written

Word of God wholeheartedly will receive perfect deliverance. You may need to deal with your religious doctrines and barriers, family limitations and abandon your Sodom before your deliverance can be affected.

Many people dine with Satan. Some live with Delilah, while others pitch their tents near Sodom and Gomorrah. There are people who swim in their affluence and spend their time in far countries. If you want true and lasting deliverance, do not give yourself access to sin, the flesh or things that oppose holiness.

Do not forget that you are in a warfare situation. You have to be in the camp of Jesus to win the battle. This is because where you are in times of warfare determines your end. You have to position yourself rightly in Christ before you can use God's resources and power to overcome the devil.

> "Then he answered and spake unto me, saying, This is the word of the LORD unto Zerubbabel, saying, Not by might, nor by power, but by my spirit, saith the LORD of hosts" (Zechariah 4:6).

> "Hast thou not known? Hast thou not heard, that the everlasting God, the LORD, the Creator of the ends of the earth, fainteth not, neither is weary? There is no searching of his understanding. He giveth power to the faint; and to them that have no might he increaseth strength. Even the youths shall faint and be weary, and the young men shall utterly fall: But they that wait upon the LORD shall renew their strength; they shall mount up with wings as eagles; they shall run, and not be weary; and they shall walk, and not faint" (Isaiah 40:28-31).

If you are going to overcome the devil, his evil spirits and agents, then you have to be spiritually strong through Jesus Christ. You may need to add fasting to your prayers. If you are already pregnant, you may pray alone in faith. Ask for divine strength so that you do not faint or be weary.

You cannot fight spiritual battles carnally or with human techniques. God has made His power available to all His children to appropriate by being obedient and putting on the whole armor of God. There are Christians who were destined for victory, but they fell on the day of battle.

> *"Be sober, be vigilant; because your adversary the devil, as a roaring lion, walketh about, seeking whom he may devour: Whom resist steadfast in the faith, knowing that the same afflictions are accomplished in your brethren that are in the world"* (1 Peter 5: 8-9).

> *"And he said unto me, My grace is sufficient for thee: for my strength is made perfect in weakness. Most gladly therefore will I rather glory in my infirmities, that the power of Christ may rest upon me"* (2 Corinthians 12:9).

Without God's grace and power of the Holy Spirit, it will be impossible for you to make it to the end. Those who are confident in themselves always fail in ordinary battles and minor temptations because they rely upon their own strength. You must vacate Satan's territory. Otherwise, he would capture you eventually. Whatever your spiritual experiences and gifting are, you must arise and reposition yourself in order to resist the devil.

"And the LORD God prepared a gourd, and made it to come up over Jonah, that it might be a shadow over his head, to deliver him from his grief. So, Jonah was exceeding glad of the gourd. But God prepared a worm when the morning rose the next day, and it smote the gourd that it withered" (Jonah 4:6-7).

"For though we walk in the flesh, we do not war after the flesh: (For the weapons of our warfare are not carnal, but mighty through God to the pulling down of strong holds;) Casting down imaginations, and every high thing that exalteth itself against the knowledge of God, and bringing into captivity every thought to the obedience of Christ" (2 Corinthians 10:3-5).

You can overcome all your enemies with spiritual weapons, which is the whole armor of God. You must be sober and vigilant, and fight as if your eternal destiny depends on your victory. Whatever you do, pray wisely. If you have to wait on the Lord a bit longer, fast and keep praying all night. Do not be mindful of your flesh, and do not take it easy on your enemy. Let your greatest concern be how to win the enemy and break the backbone of all the powers behind your problems.

"Thou therefore endure hardness, as a good soldier of Jesus Christ. No man that warreth entangleth himself with the affairs of this life; that he may please him who hath chosen him to be a soldier" (2 Timothy 2:3-4).

"For the love of money is the root of all evil: which while some coveted after, they have erred from the faith, and pierced themselves through with many sorrows. But thou, O man of God, flee these

things; and follow after righteousness, godliness, faith, love, patience, meekness. Fight the good fight of faith, lay hold on eternal life, where unto thou art also called, and hast professed a good profession before many witnesses" (1 Timothy 6:10-12).

Separate yourself from every distraction and other issues. Apportion enough time to fight against problems that bother your life. Two armies cannot fight and win decisively at the same time. Satan has to lose and God has to win.

Jacob separated himself from the affairs of this world in order to settle with Esau finally. Free yourself from temporary enjoyment, youthful lusts and vehemently strive to set yourself free from bondage.

"Wherefore seeing we also are compassed about with so great a cloud of witnesses, let us lay aside every weight, and the sin which doth so easily beset us, and let us run with patience the race that is set before us, Looking unto Jesus the author and finisher of our faith; who for the joy that was set before him endured the cross, despising the shame, and is set down at the right hand of the throne of God. For consider him that endured such contradiction of sinners against himself, lest ye be wearied and faint in your minds. Ye have not yet resisted unto blood, striving against sin" (Hebrews 12:1-4).

"But I say unto you, That whosoever looketh on a woman to lust after her hath committed adultery with her already in his heart. And if thy right eye offend thee, pluck it out, and cast it from thee: for it is profitable for thee that one of thy members should perish, and not that thy whole body should

10

be cast into hell. And if thy right hand offend thee, cut it off, and cast it from thee: for it is profitable for thee that one of thy members should perish, and not that thy whole body should be cast into hell" (<u>Matthew 5:28-30</u>).

"Dearly beloved, I beseech you as strangers and pilgrims, abstain from fleshly lusts, which war against the soul" (<u>1 Peter 2:11</u>).

What you stand to gain if you win the battle is much more. Stand and fight for your right strongly and your enemies would surrender. Cut off every source of distraction, temptation and as much as it lays in your power, resist the devil.

Persistence, faith and resistance are common to all winners no matter their experiences. Our life on earth is short and the challenge before us is for us to face the enemy now. You have a life to live and if you must, it has to be to the glory of God who has created you for His glory. Do not die at the mercy of the devil. If you were able to get married, then you will also be able to have children. God is able.

"And not only they, but ourselves also, which have the first fruits of the Spirit, even we ourselves groan within ourselves, waiting for the adoption, to wit, the redemption of our body" (<u>Romans 8:23</u>).

PUT ON THE WHOLE ARMOR OF GOD

God, the Father of all blessings, made His power to get victory over Satan and the world available to all His children. He knew that there is a spiritual battle going on. That was why God did not want us to be vulnerable to the attacks of the devil. This is the reason why wise and victorious Christians put on the whole armor of God always. Otherwise, the devil would pull you down by any means. This is a wakeup call for you to rise up and put on the whole armor of God as the Scripture advised us to do in order to resist the devil successfully.

> *"Finally, my brethren, be strong in the Lord, and in the power of his might. Put on the whole armor of God, that ye may be able to stand against the wiles of the devil. For we wrestle not against flesh and blood, but against principalities, against powers, against the rulers of the darkness of this world, against spiritual wickedness in high* places. *Wherefore take unto you the whole armor of God that ye may be able to withstand in the evil day, and having done all, to stand. Stand therefore, having your loins girt about with truth, and having on the breastplate of righteousness; And your feet shod with the preparation of the gospel of peace; Above all, taking the shield of faith, wherewith ye shall be able to quench all the fiery darts of the wicked. And take the helmet of salvation, and the sword of the Spirit, which is the word of God"* (Ephesians 6:10-17).

All things are possible with God. Therefore, be strong in Him. If you would stand out as one of the victors in this generation, you must to wrestle against principalities, powers and rulers of darkness of this world and against spiritual wickedness on high places successfully. You need God's amour in these evil days. I want you to note carefully the importance of each of the parts of the armor of God.

THE BELT OF TRUTH

Having the belt of truth is standing on what you know is right and insisting on doing things the right way. You must pattern your life according to all truth as revealed in the written Word of God.

> *"Wherefore gird up the loins of your mind, be sober, and hope to the end for the grace that is to be brought unto you at the revelation of Jesus Christ"* (1 Peter 1:13).

Do not allow problems to sway your mind from the truth. It is always easy to drift off. Always look at the bigger picture of life, where all things are working out for good to them that love God. Hold on to the truth with hope and you will overcome.

THE BREAST PLATE OF RIGHTEOUSNESS

Usually during desert or storm experiences, Satan knows how to open many doors of escape. Even when such doors appear certain to offer solace, shun those doors and keep in the way of righteousness. Maintain your relationship with Christ and He will not abandon you.

> *"As obedient children, not fashioning yourselves according to the former lusts in your ignorance: But as he which hath called you is holy, so be ye holy in all manner of conversation; Because it is written, Be ye holy; for I am holy"* (1 Peter 1:14-16).

Remain in your obedience to the Word of God and refuse to look back or compromise your faith in Christ. Holiness must be your goal strictly in order to win the enemy at the end. Devil will send many evil messengers to get you off track, but take a stand and remain on the path of righteousness.

"And your feet shod with the preparation of the gospel of peace" (Ephesians 6:15).

THE SHOES OF THE GOSPEL OF PEACE

Establish your feet on the Word of God. Do not accept anything that contradicts the gospel of peace. The devil has a way offering deliverance that can bring temporary peace. However, insist on the gospel of peace that is rooted on God's Word as Paul did.

"For I am not ashamed of the gospel of Christ: for it is the power of God unto salvation to everyone that believeth; to the Jew first, and also to the Greek. For therein is the righteousness of God revealed from faith to faith: as it is written, The just shall live by faith" (Romans 1:16-17).

Barrenness, miscarriage and reproach may stir you in your face, yet, do not let any of them sway your faith and trust in the gospel of Jesus. Clothe yourself with the gospel of peace. The devil has deceived many people with fake blessings that brought them sorrow, pains and eternal damnation. Therefore, do not allow temporary shame, reproach or disgrace to force you into accepting the devil's solution.

Trust in the power of God that can bring true blessings without sorrow. That is why the gospel of Christ said that the just shall live by faith.

15

THE SHIELD OF FAITH

Faith is the key that unlocks the doors of heavenly resources and prayer without faith is useless. The Scriptures reckoned that great men subdued kingdoms through faith:

> *"And what shall I more say? For the time would fail me to tell of Gedeon, and of Barak, and of Samson, and of Jephthae; of David also, and Samuel, and of the prophets: Who through faith subdued kingdoms, wrought righteousness, obtained promises, stopped the mouths of lions, Quenched the violence of fire, escaped the edge of the sword, out of weakness were made strong, waxed valiant in fight, turned to flight the armies of the aliens"* (Hebrews 11:32-34)

> *"Whom resist steadfast in the faith, knowing that the same afflictions are accomplished in your brethren that are in the world"* (1 Peter 5:9).

> *"For whatsoever is born of God overcometh the world: and this is the victory that overcometh the world, even our faith"* (1 John 5:4).

If you have been praying, have faith. Trust in God's Word that He may answer your prayers. You can subdue kingdoms through faith. Evil forces that resist your conception, or cause you to suffer barrenness, miscarriage and abortion could be the kingdoms that are standing before you. If mighty men could subdue their kingdoms through faith, then you can also subdue yours through faith.

God is not partial, so believe Him and see your own kingdom subdued. The powers that resist your prayers now have done the same to others in the past.

16

Therefore, do not allow any particular problem to shift your faith from Christ.

The shield of faith quenches or extinguishes the fieriest darts of the enemy. The devil fire arrows of impurity, selfishness, doubt, fear, discouragement, unbelief and many evil thoughts to dislodge your faith and focus on Christ. Use the shield of faith to defend yourself.

THE HELMET OF SALVATION

Salvation is deliverance and preservation from evil, sin and the consequence of the fall of man. It is the foundation pillar of the gospel. Without salvation, everything else is useless and worst than nothing. It is a priceless treasure that devil is willing to offer anything on earth in exchange of it. Devil can promise you a child, prosperity or even the whole world in exchange of your salvation. However, remember that nothing on earth is worth the price of your salvation.

> *"And take the helmet of salvation, and the sword of the Spirit, which is the word of God"* (Ephesians 6:17).

> *"But let us, who are of the day, be sober, putting on the breastplate of faith and love; and for a helmet, the hope of salvation"* (1 Thessalonians 5:8).

A Roman soldier would never go into battle without putting his helmet on. The helmet protects the head from arrows and broadsword. You must resist anything that draws you back to sin. This is because evil arrows are capable of wasting your destiny and commit your soul to hell. The battle will soon be over, so do not allow unbelief from the devil and his agents to abort your salvation.

THE SWORD OF THE SPIRIT

"And the LORD spake unto Moses and unto Aaron, saying, Take the sum of the sons of Kohath from among the sons of Levi, after their families, by the house of their fathers, From thirty years old and upward even until fifty years old, all that enter into the host, to do the work in the tabernacle of the congregation. This shall be the service of the sons of Kohath in the tabernacle of the congregation, about the most holy things: And when the camp setteth forward, Aaron shall come, and his sons, and they shall take down the covering vail, and cover the ark of testimony with it: And shall put thereon the covering of badgers' skins, and shall spread over it a cloth wholly of blue, and shall put in the staves thereof. And upon the table of showbread they shall spread a cloth of blue, and put thereon the dishes, and the spoons, and the bowls, and covers to cover withal: and the continual bread shall be thereon: And they shall spread upon them a cloth of scarlet, and cover the same with a covering of badgers' skins, and shall put in the staves thereof. And they shall take a cloth of blue, and cover the candlestick of the light, and his lamps, and his tongs, and his snuff dishes, and all the oil vessels thereof, wherewith they minister unto it: And they shall put it and all the vessels thereof within a covering of badgers' skins, and shall put it upon a bar. And upon the golden altar they shall spread a cloth of blue, and cover it with a covering of badgers' skins, and shall put to the staves thereof" (Numbers 4:1-11).

> *"Thy word have I hid in mine heart, that I might not sin against thee"* (Psalms 119:11)

God's Word makes us wiser than the cleverest tempter. If the devil could surrender when Jesus quoted God's Word, then he would also surrender as you keep quoting the Word of God. Obedience to God's Word at all times will go a long way to prepare you for victory.

> *"For the word of God is quick, and powerful, and sharper than any two-edged sword, piercing even to the dividing asunder of soul and spirit, and of the joints and marrow, and is a discerner of the thoughts and intents of the heart"* (Hebrews 4:12).

> *"But sanctify the Lord God in your hearts: and be ready always to give an answer to every man that asketh you a reason of the hope that is in you with meekness and fear"* (1 Peter 3:15).

The devil may tempt you through the corruption of your heart, or entice you through your eyes or through your carelessness. Temptation can come through what you love most. It could be an idol in your mind. You must fight your battle with the sword of the spirit (Rhema), which is specific utterance of God. There is always a specific Word of God for every temptation. God's armor is powerful enough to help you overcome every problem and keep your pregnancy. Therefore, trust in His Word.

POWERS THAT TERMINATE PREGNANCIES

The bible revealed that devil's (your enemy) mission is to steal, kill and destroy. Therefore, is it hard for you to understand that there are evil powers that seek to terminate pregnancies? Devil's chief work is to oppose God, His works and children, and to counterfeit everything that God created.

> *"¹⁰And Moses and Aaron went in unto Pharaoh, and they did so as the LORD had commanded: and Aaron cast down his rod before Pharaoh, and before his servants, and it became a serpent. ¹¹Then Pharaoh also called the wise men and the sorcerers: now the magicians of Egypt, they also did in like manner with their enchantments. ¹²For they cast down every man his rod, and they became serpents: but Aaron's rod swallowed up their rods. ¹³And he hardened Pharaoh's heart that he hearkened not unto them; as the LORD had said. ²⁰And Moses and Aaron did so, as the LORD commanded; and he lifted up the rod, and smote the waters that were in the river, in the sight of Pharaoh, and in the sight of his servants; and all the waters that were in the river were turned to blood. ²¹And the fish that was in the river died; and the river stank, and the Egyptians could not drink of the water of the river; and there was blood throughout all the land of Egypt. ²²And the magicians of Egypt did so with their enchantments: and Pharaoh's heart was hardened, neither did he hearken unto them; as the LORD had said"* (Exodus 7:10-13, 20-22).

The devil knows how to counterfeit God's work. He creates counterfeit of every genuine thing God created,

20

in order to confuse men and deceive those who desire to serve God. People who consult agents of devil in order to get pregnant are taking a dangerous risk. Many false prophets are parading themselves as solution providers and ignorant people are going to ask for their prophecies, prayers and blessings to get children. If you want godly children, stay in the Word of God. Often, some prophecies come true. However, you should run away when prophets and ministers of the gospel start demanding that you do anything that contradicts the Word of God.

> *"And it came to pass on the morrow, that the evil spirit from God came upon Saul, and he prophesied in the midst of the house: and David played with his hand, as at other times: and there was a javelin in Saul's hand. And Saul cast the javelin; for he said, I will smite David even to the wall with it. And David avoided out of his presence twice"* (1 Samuel 18:10-11).

> *"He cried also in mine ears with a loud voice, saying, Cause them that have charge over the city to draw near, even every man with his destroying weapon in his hand. And, behold, six men came from the way of the higher gate, which lieth toward the north, and every man a slaughter weapon in his hand; and one man among them was clothed with linen, with a writer's inkhorn by his side: and they went in, and stood beside the brasen altar. And the glory of the God of Israel was gone up from the cherub, whereupon he was, to the threshold of the house. And he called to the man clothed with linen, which had the writer's inkhorn by his side; And the LORD said unto him, Go through the midst of the city, through the midst of Jerusalem, and set a mark upon the foreheads of the men that sigh and that cry for all the*

abominations that be done in the midst thereof" (Ezekiel 9:1-4).

Many miracle workers today are disguised agents of Satan. They perform wonders but they do not have the likeness of God in their lives. They prophesy to people, but secretly hate God's children and plan for their deaths. They claim to be prophets and holy men and women of God while the works of the flesh rule their lives.

> *"Now the works of the flesh are manifest, which are these; Adultery, fornication, uncleanness, lasciviousness, Idolatry, witchcraft, hatred, variance, emulations, wrath, strife, seditions, heresies, Envyings, murders, drunkenness, revellings, and such like: of the which I tell you before, as I have also told you in time past, that they which do such things shall not inherit the kingdom of God"* (Galatians 5:19-21).

They cannot control their fleshly desires. They commit adultery, fornication and worship idols. They envy and murder innocent people, yet they perform deceptive wonders. The devil is at work through these false apostles and deceivers, who transformed themselves into apostles of Christ.

> *"For such are false apostles, deceitful workers, transforming themselves into the apostles of Christ. And no marvel; for Satan himself is transformed into an angel of light. Therefore it is no great thing if his ministers also be transformed as the ministers of righteousness; whose end shall be according to their works"* (2 Corinthians 11:13-15).

Many of these prophets are like Samson who did not know that the Spirit of God has departed from him. Whenever you notice any sign of greed, pride, unforgiving spirit, immorality, jealousy, anger, covetousness, unfaithfulness in the family, financial irresponsibility, etc., in any of these so-called miracle workers, know that the devil is in-charge.

When sin sits on the throne of a man's life, all, which is left, is fake and unprofitable. These groups of people are Satan's agents. They want to destroy your pregnancy. They want to shut your womb. Devil can insert an arrow of death in a womb to remain permanently barren. Satanic agents can influence children in the womb to convert them to strange children. They can target an organ of the body, injure unborn babies or place evil marks upon people. Do not visit places where satanic agents present themselves as ministers of solutions. Nevertheless, if you have done so, you need some prayers of deliverance.

> *"Another parable put he forth unto them, saying, The kingdom of heaven is likened unto a man which sowed good seed in his field: But while men slept, his enemy came and sowed tares among the wheat, and went his way"* (<u>Matthew 13:24-25</u>).

Another deadly enemy of women during pregnancy is evil dream. This is when devil begins to attack women through their dreams. When he feeds a pregnant woman in the dream or shows her red things, miscarriage would take place, if she does not pray effective prayers. But such shall not be your portion in the name of Jesus.

> *"Send thine hand from above; rid me, and deliver me out of great waters, from the hand of strange children"* (<u>Psalms 144:7</u>).

23

> *"And when he came to him, behold, he stood by his burnt offering, and the princes of Moab with him. And Balak said unto him, What hath the LORD spoken?"* (Numbers 23:17).

There was a case where evil agents summoned a womb and placed it at their altar to control the pregnancy. They can raise spirit husband or wife from their altars or invoke a spirit from your place of birth to marry you spiritually.

> *"⁶And the angels which kept not their first estate, but left their own habitation, he hath reserved in everlasting chains under darkness unto the judgment of the great day. ⁸Likewise also these* filthy *dreamers defile the flesh, despise dominion, and speak evil of dignities"* (Jude 1:6, 8)

Do not take food and sex you have in the dreams lightly because they are not ordinary. Evil dreams, eating, drinking, sex and other demonic activities in the dream have negative consequences. Evil things that could happen through dreams include:

- Inflicting a woman with a strange sickness that affects pregnancies.

- The killing, stealing or destroying of the destiny of the baby in the womb (Acts 16:16, 18-19).

- Depression, weakness and strange tiredness that discourage people to pray more.

- Sudden disaster or miscarriage.

- Abnormal bleeding, plantation of fibroid and evil growth.

24

- Induced hatred, rejection, marital problems and divorce.

- Premature or prolonged labor and birth.

- Incision of evil marks, curse or spell.

- Strange problems and events.

As a wise woman, you must pray seriously during your pregnancies. Your prayers can keep your baby safe, break evil padlocks, chains, and deliver your unborn baby from witchcraft attacks.

PRAYERS TO RETAIN YOUR PREGNANCY

Bible references: <u>Exodus 23:25</u>; <u>Deuteronomy 28:1-14</u>

Begin with praise and worship

1. Every agent of miscarriage in my life, die, in the name of Jesus.

2. Every messenger of abortion in my life, carry your message to your sender, in the name of Jesus.

3. Agent of premature death to my pregnancy, be frustrated, in the name of Jesus.

4. Let every weak part of my womb receive power, in the name of Jesus.

5. I command the eaters of the flesh and the drinkers of blood to die, in the name of Jesus.

6. I command every agent of affliction against my pregnancy to be terminated, in the name of Jesus.

7. Any evil priest that has vowed to terminate my pregnancy, be disgraced, in the name of Jesus.

8. Every arrow of death that is fired at my pregnancy, backfire, in the name of Jesus.

9. Blood of Jesus deliver my pregnancy from the reach of evil spies, in the name of Jesus.

10. Any power that is manipulating my pregnancy, die, in the name of Jesus.

11. I command every power that has arrested my pregnancy to release it by force, in the name of Jesus.

12. Any evil altar that is attacking my pregnancy, scatter by fire, in the name of Jesus.

13. I paralyze any satanic minister that was assigned to minister to my pregnancy, in the name of Jesus.

14. Let the power of the grave that has buried my pregnancy break to pieces, in the name of Jesus.

15. I reject evil summons that was issued to my pregnancy, in the name of Jesus.

16. Every evil observer that is monitoring my pregnancy, die, in the name of Jesus.

17. I cleanse all witchcraft handwritings over my pregnancy with the blood of Jesus, in the name of Jesus.

18. I reverse satanic arrows that were fired at my pregnancy, in the name of Jesus.

19. I command every satanic bullet that entered my pregnancy to come out by force, in the name of Jesus.

20. I cast out every spirit of tragedy that was programmed to my pregnancy, in the name of Jesus.

21. Any evil covenant that is working against my pregnancy, break to pieces, in the name of Jesus.

22. Any curse that is prevailing over my pregnancy, expire by force, in the name of Jesus.

23. I wipe out all evil marks on my pregnancy, in the name of Jesus.

24. I destroy any power that was assigned to amputate my pregnancy, in the name of Jesus.

25. Any evil personality that is contending with my pregnancy, die, in the name of Jesus.

26. Every dark agent that is promoting abortion in my life, be disgraced, in the name of Jesus.

27. Any evil voice that is announcing my pregnancy, I silence you forever, in the name of Jesus.

28. Let the killers of pregnancies be arrested and destroyed by fire, in the name of Jesus.

29. I terminate any evil advertisement that is advertising my pregnancy, in the name of Jesus.

30. I command any evil program that is going on for my pregnancy to stop, in the name of Jesus.

31. Any attack on my pregnancy through my dreams, be frustrated, in the name of Jesus.

32. I demobilize any evil movement that is going on against my pregnancy, in the name of Jesus.

33. Let evil prophecies fail on the account of my pregnancy, in the name of Jesus.

34. Any evil conversion over my pregnancy, fail woefully, in the name of Jesus.

35. Every evil deposit that is made over pregnancy, I uproot you by fire, in the name of Jesus.

36. I destroy every pregnancy killer on a mission to terminate my pregnancy, in the name of Jesus.

37. Every unprofitable load that sits upon my pregnancy, drop by force, in the name of Jesus.

38. Let evil reinforcements to attack my pregnancy scatter in shame, in the name of Jesus.

Thank You So Much!

Beloved, I hope you enjoyed this book as much as I believe God has touched your heart today. I cannot thank you enough for your continued support for this prayer ministry.

I appreciate you so much for taking out time to read this wonderful prayer book, and if you have an extra second, I would love to hear what you think about this book.

Please, do share your testimonies with me by sending emails to pastor@prayermadueke.com, or through the social media at www.facebook.com/prayer.madueke. I invite you also to www.prayermadueke.com to view other books I have written on various issues of life, especially on marriage, family, sexual problems and money.

I will be delighted to partner with you in organized crusades, ceremonies, marriages and Marriage seminars, special events, church ministration and fellowship for the advancement of God's Kingdom here on earth.

Thank you again, and I wish you success in your life.

God bless you.

In Christ,

Prayer M. Madueke

OTHER BOOKS BY PRAYER M. MADUEKE

- *21/40 Nights Of Decrees And Your Enemies Will Surrender*
- *Confront And Conquer*
- *Tears in Prison*
- *35 Special Dangerous Decrees*
- *The Reality of Spirit Marriage*
- *Queen of Heaven*
- *Leviathan the Beast*
- *100 Days Prayer To Wake Up Your Lazarus*
- *Dangerous Decrees To Destroy Your Destroyers*
- *The spirit of Christmas*
- *More Kingdoms To Conquer*
- *Your Dream Directory*
- *The Sword Of New Testament Deliverance*
- *Alphabetic Battle For Unmerited Favors*
- *Alphabetic Character Deliverance*
- *Holiness*
- *The Witchcraft Of The Woman That Sits Upon Many Waters*
- *The Operations Of The Woman That Sits Upon Many Waters*
- *Powers To Pray Once And Receive Answers*
- *Prayer Riots To Overthrow Divorce*
- *Prayers To Get Married Happily*
- *Prayers To Keep Your Marriage Out of Troubles*
- *Prayers For Conception And Power To Retain*
- *Prayer Retreat – Prayers to Possess Your Year*
- *Prayers for Nation Building*
- *Organized student in a disorganized school*
- *Welcome to Campus*
- *Alone with God (10 series)*

31

CONTACTS

AFRICA
#1 Babatunde close,
Off Olaitan Street, Surulere
Lagos, Nigeria
+234 803 353 0599
pastor@prayermadueke.com

#Plot 1791, No. 3 Ijero Close,
Flat 2, Area 1,
Garki 1 - FCT, Abuja
+234 807 065 4159

IRELAND
Ps Emmanuel Oko
#84 Thornfield Square
Cloudalkin D22
Ireland
Tel: +353 872 820 909, +353 872 977 422
aghaoko2003@yahoo.com

EUROPE/SCHENGEN
Collins Kwame
#46 Felton Road
Barking
Essex IG11 7XZ GB
Tel: +44 208 507 8083, +44 787 703 2386, +44 780 703 6916
aghaoko2003@yahoo.com

Printed in Great Britain
by Amazon

62157415R00024